SOUND FURY

SOUND FURY

poems by Mark Levine

University of Iowa Press /// Iowa City

University of Iowa Press, Iowa City 52242
Copyright © 2022 by Mark Levine
uipress.uiowa.edu
Printed in the United States of America
Design by Sara T. Sauers
Printed on acid-free paper

Library of Congress Cataloging-in-Publication Data
Names: Levine, Mark, 1965– author.
Title: Sound Fury: Poems / Mark Levine.
Description: Iowa City: University of Iowa Press, 2022.
Identifiers: LCCN 2022006314 (print) | LCCN 2022006315 (ebook) |
    ISBN 9781609388690 (paperback; acid-free paper) |
    ISBN 9781609388706 (ebook)
Subjects: LCGFT: Poetry.
Classification: LCC PS3562.E8978 S68 2022 (print) |
    LCC PS3562.E8978 (ebook) | DDC 811/.54—dc23/eng/20220225
LC record available at https://lccn.loc.gov/2022006314
LC ebook record available at https://lccn.loc.gov/2022006315

TO MY TEACHERS

Philip Levine
Michael S. Harper
Jorie Graham
James Galvin

CONTENTS

By force to ravish, or by fraud betray.

—ALEXANDER POPE, "The Rape of the Lock"

He knew that in the cubicle next to him the little woman with sandy hair toiled day in, day out, simply at tracking down and deleting from the press the names of people who had been vaporized and were therefore considered never to have existed. There was a certain fitness in this, since her own husband had been vaporized a couple of years earlier. And a few cubicles away a mild, ineffectual, dreamy creature named Ampleforth, with very hairy ears and a surprising talent for juggling with rhymes and meters, was engaged in producing garbled versions— definitive texts, they were called—of poems which had become ideologically offensive but which for one reason or another were to be retained in the anthologies.

—GEORGE ORWELL, 1984

SOUND FURY

Lark

Storm of storms: We slept through it
In a golden stupor. True, it
Did its damage before it withdrew. It
Emptied our orchard of unharvested fruit
Along with a fruit-picking crew it
Hurled hither and yon, bushels askew; it
Did not apologize, either, though a few it-
Ty bitty groans slipped through it-
S pores, a sorrowful fugue. It
Remained, elsewise, mute.
Indifferent to logic or pleas—betraying no clue it
Had sunk in us a dream of harsh rescue—it
Washed the sky in a cascading blue it
Called "Midnight Curfew." It
Fell to us, wee ones, to prosecute
Our case against it; to pursue it-
S condemnation, issue it
Formal summonses, eschew it
Publicly but proportionately and put the screws to it
Before its germ spread beyond the few it
Counted as footmen: That fleet fellow Pruitt,
Tongue-snarler; his hirsute It-
Alo-Romanian strongboy, Radu, it-
Emizer of dark expenses; and the pet Jew, It-
Zhak, with whom it spun a dashing minuet.
Had we grown a touch too it
-Chy with grievance? We stepped back to review it
And ourselves through it
S scuzzy screen—astute brute,
Trouncer of the food/sex/feces/corpse-defiling taboo it
Drew it
S power from—and ask what restitut-

Ion was due it.

Did we crave to lure it to remnant woods, queue it

Up and spill goo into it?

Yes; but we lacked the wherewithal to go through w/ it.

It languished in a cage of bamboo it

Mocked as a mighty tower; too, it

Resisted all efforts to woo it

With savory treats, choosing to chew it-

S moony fingernails down to the root,

Awaiting its debut. It

Gave commands and bade us hop to it,

Grubbing holy text only to strew it

-S pages like fumes up the flue it

Snapped shut on us. Ours was a fluid

Situation, no will to praise or to rue it,

Clarify or misconstrue it

S motives. Time was—as we once knew it—

An enemy came and our soldier slew it

Without hesitation in absolute

Righteous rage. This was a new it

Eration. What matter why or how or who it

Was had fallen among us?—or if it was me or you it

Aimed to undo? It

Advised us to get used to it

S'presence, whistling a plucky off-tune *Alouette*

In our sleepless faces and dousing us with dew it

Mustered night and day like suet.

What next, old coot?

There was more than nothing to it.

Untitled (Sir)

Uncomprehending, overwhelming, combative
Regressive, regretful, insincere
Engulfed, disgraced, contrary, forgotten
Misbegotten, misshapen, miscellaneous mister.
Unscrupulous, overweening comrade-in-arms.
Regicidal regimental insectivore.
Englishman dispatched convivially forth,
Misty missile misfiring mischievously.
Underwater ovum combing
Regal regions inland.
Engine disbursing countrified fucks
Misleads meshugana Miss Mishkin.
Missing-the-mark, misery mistakes miso
For continental dish engendering
Insubordinate regurgitas—pregnancy—
Combustible overcoats—until
Dingdong: Helmeted wombats
Caress egrets, sinkholes.
Fried rice condoms go
Begging apes for cellophane terraria.
U owe community
Wreathes, rental-income, inch-long
Engravings your racist corpse forges.
Miss us, miscreant? Miss missing?
Apprehensive, well-meaning, we've
Aggressively retched in sync,
Unfed, effaced, eerily gotten,
Gotten by happenstance, skeletally, Sir!

Sacrificial

The sight was unholy
In unruly ways: An ungainly
Splayed-toed ungulate
Leisurely lending its hide
To an unshod legion
Of relief-seekers
Encamped luridly
On the leeward side
Of cowardly Uncle Al's
Leafy onion patch.
That was a way of saying that
We swatted gnats
From the boss man's ashcan
Uncannily, for his cinders
Fetched a fee
Of umpteen tokens
Allegedly, and we were
Ungodly poor for purposes
Obscure as rubber.
The latest downpour
Unsheltered us, as
The one before squandered us
Under riverine skies
For all to see our rug-rash and tats
Uneasily. Understand,
Dundering refugees and
Blunt-barreled escapees sunned
Themselves elegiacally
On the majesty's airstrip's runway
Like a hundred and one
Junked souls, while
Unnameable entities

Scrabbled for undue
Credit in abundant
Elsewhere's darkness.
Unseemly, yes; unlikely, no.
Our broom-pusher
Misses no unsightly spot
Umbrellas cannot reach,
Oh lonely love's labor.
Hungrily and angrily
We chew our scud
In the holding pen, like
Undocumented legal
Umbilici, voted most likely
To be packed in ice.

Sound Fury

Big boys in big rigs
Hoisting dying cigarettes by moonlight:
The jig is up, the long-embargoed airtight freighter
Has run zigzaggingly aground,
Turning our ignition all off.
It was a good gig in its day, pouring forth
Our frightened hearts to birds—
Jackdaws, indigo buntings, solemn
Nightingales and migratory wingers
Alighting on tundra and taiga.
We strummed madrigals, stomped gigues.
We lived on chump change and indignity,
Ambiguous prayer, smidgens of self-regard, ignominious
Sighs in the twigs behind the marketplace
Where cockfighters crouched
And significant amigos blustered, swigging
From watery dark spigots;
While a loose-lipped prodigal
Piggie asquat in our doorsill recalled falling
Into a crossfire one piquant Paraguayan night
And finding religion
Bigtime: We saw his bushy effigy
Rise on a flagpole, poignantly aflutter,
As his body ran off with the neighbor lady's
Obliging negligee, and it was all
We could not do to giggle.
He was not the only foreigner among us,
The only aboriginal, or bigot,
Unpedigreed lamplighter lost
In a lonesome impulse of delight
With a canteenful of pungent tiger juice
Snagged in his riggings,

Fit for gigantic thirst. Like us,
He was hunting down transfiguration, go
Figure, and had irrigated a frontier or two
In his campaign to litigate
The intransigent Signifier.
What starry signals signaled he?—
Who digressed incorrigibly, assigning blame
For his portfolio of malign designs
To the Ministry of Intelligence,
The frigging god-sucking sovereign.
It was our unmitigated lot to bed down
With earwigs and fleas in what few corners
Of his brig remained unnavigated;
A splendid assignation.
Thus it was insight flamed out in us.
The sundry sky, the eight-fingered tendrils
Of our obligatory houseplant, were
Enigmas to us; the beach we washed up on
Ran with fatigued waterfowl,
Jetsam and sewerage, unfumigated
Pips digging for bony messengers in the tide.
Where must one turn one's might
When one's fond figments go
Poof? We have no epigraph
To pen; no trigger to caress.
It is curtain time for Figaro and his zaftig bride-to-be
In the stone age of enlightenment in the
Coign of courtly intrigue.
Vertigo is the paradigm.
What stagehand deigns to designate our hero
A squealing prig, and a tragic
Closet bigamist to boot?

The Vision

Sitting alone, as one forsook,
Wasted and dull, I pried a book
From the tight pocket where it kept
My company by day, and schlepped
Me town to town, indifferently,
By night. Strange friend it was to me . . .
A little tome, whose hushed address
Stirred in me visions of undress,
Of calves, and colts, and other young
Creatures one yearned to rove among.
Pictures there were, too—faint—and a fair
Snippet of downy yearling hair
Tucked softly midst the ample prose.
Such fearful impulses arose!—
Which could not be neglected, try
Forcefully though I might to deny
My state of bodily distress.
But now the State comes for redress.
It finds me cowering here, and shunned;
And holds my disgraced poet's hand
To its impartial correcting stove:
Herrick, you are too coarse to love.

The Argument of His Book

Tell how little Brooksy's pissing stunt teed off the minyan
This morning at Holy Blossom Temple in Toronto, Ont., deep
Downstream from Dad's coma: Tell how Flora Bird kept the adolescent
Pews amused with her annealing powers, supplying wet blessings
To "those who know who they are" who opened their wallets last April
To fortify Sy Goldfarb, Mayor of Mitzvah
And his jejune platoon, of blessed memory.
"Tell how you lie to us, little chicken hawk, when you plead with us
To hide your ashes in a box of Maypo
Lenore Braverman packed up for you" squawks the Rebbe in our direction
In chopped tongue: See, our tribe was in hock to the cart-man's
Skin collectors long centuries ago, see; holy snow assailed us
On the mount and wooden paddles would not wake us and
For this we smash our kishkas in your ratty cab ride?
Dolus specialis: The well-dressed fella grooms us for a float
Down today's white pride parade, brandishing in the gutter
His fat bridle. "Baby cakes"
(He hums), "my youth is spent,
And a mouthful of wanton necessity it was
To share such fondues/With the likes of youz."
Ransomed wads are thusly offered
Unto the outspread paralyzed palms upon which our
Pocked cheeks balance, and though we would not spoil the ending
We would not spice it up for you either, god willing,
Miss Anna Banana: Your words could use a little limberness
Rehearsing your pantomime in the front man's Trans Am,
Shifting for the feel of it, can you feel it, how does it feel?
Hedgerows, hardly hedgerows, sporty hemlines
Split down the seams with a mighty case of dreads
At Aunt Lily's ranch house on Carmichael that night
Mom is set to expire and take her white lies
With her to the grove with the plates you busted, you get me?
My god, I cannot find my people in the twilight searchlight

In their flammable ginghams, yet
When we open our eyes we are all aboard the Kingston ferry
With no Gravol for queasy aunts and uncles and dead pets
And you listen, little mister smarty-pants, you are asking for it,
Asking a survivor to drop you off in Hell
At the front curb where we just may interrupt our heaving for you
After all we've done for you.

(for Grandpa)

Ornery

Man comes crying cause
His shit's been stolen
Underfoot while hard
At leisure, strung
Out and bobbing
Like clubbed rockfish
In a depthless pool
Hung with hurling
Stalactites and gnarled
Roots of ficus and fruit
Bats eking it out.
Flip-flops float fearlessly as
Man comes toweling his
Dripping self off
The limey ledge
All lost in breezeless
Panic up a moss-
Slimed crow's nest and
Smoked out: Now
What he wouldn't do
For a stiff one
Man, to bring himself back
Man, cause his shit
Stole off down current
Out to sea, come
Away, man.
Sunburnt heels hobble homeward
In strange shoes as moonlight
Goes silent as a wreck.
All climb one crumby temple
All see the likeness
Of two mean-tempered curs

Poking out treetops
Like elbows. All look down
Down down
All see a mound
Rising of scrub drug
Off by jungle solitaires
Wearing shadows like leaves.
Man moons on
And his tail hides itself
Away in high branches
Crying, crying
But more like a moan.
In appetite and
Aptitude his animal
Is just like man but
Invisible.

Bantam

These times we cannot tell our children
From chickens below, it's the same action
Neck down to the spindly hocks
They pick their way home
Uphill, feathery
Shadows on a white path, slinging
Sticks and throat-calls
Half-committed to memory
To satisfy taskmasters, masters
Of chewing, spitting up, cackling, chewing.
What marvel their memory is, the small-brained ones, the
Knotted word-strands they recover and play back
Absent meaning, scratched out in time as
They spin on hard little toes, topping
Cinder blocks and bounding against mesh
That separates our enclosure
From animals below.
No detail escapes them—not the pied wart
Beneath Old Lady's eye
Nor the lagging stride of the wing-torn
Pullet, nor the cock's mechanical babbling
As it haunts a path, awaiting
Its drunk defeated owner
Purple crest aflame.
Then too the scrawny one
Absent from play, sullen
In duff, refusing to stir
When children kick it
"My children, my children" (we say)
"Who see everything and know nothing
Within your kingdom
Ignorant masters, suffering
Neither birth nor destiny, starving beasts"

To the Virgins, to Make Much of Time

Gatherings of men and boys went forth, and I gather
Major Robinson attended with his battered bags and his dismay.
Old Doc Hooper could not contain curses, the mottled scold,
Flying off the handle and delivering his mutt a full-on flaying,
Andante-like. Meanwhile toothy Tillotson reached for the hand
Davy's princely boy extended toward the icebox in hunger today,
Two fingers at a time. Fluorescents hummed a plaintive salute to
Undying Uncle Lemuel in his corner, blubbering on about local lads dying
Thermally in the decommissioned cesspit nigh. "How I loathe
Sons-of-bitches with dull hawsers harassing Bosun
Theo in the engine room," shrilled Keck, but our joy in the
Getting-the-filthy-job-done prevailed. It was a way of forgetting
The morning we arrived, beardless and bent sideways with the
Runs, just in time to find Stein putting a pounding on that runt
Anderson in the showers. Chewing our nails, closing eyes and
Setting down power tools—true, it was a touch upsetting
Thatcher could burst in and peel away body stockings just like that;
Thirsty fellow, officious preener, wagging his thick attaché. At first
When we consorted with honchos a sedative twilight set in, when
Warmer-blooded animals lay their hides on us and night got warmer.
But we no longer think about it—the drenched spiny sleep—but
Worst of all were Flynn's stinking boots on our pillows like bratwurst.
Times darkened. The sky ran heavy with discharge, and pastimes—
Former childhood spoils and riffs—fizzled. El Güero showed up, The Reformer,
Then came bouts of market discipline, blurts, spurts, seizures, then
Time and again young Kim, Deputy Spence's chap, turned down a good time
And reappeared later at the Solicitor's Club, jacked-up, having given his hand
Martially to the firm of Kipling & Benz, who banged him but good. In summary
Forbidden futures were traded—cancer, influence, capital, shame—before
Primeval winds snatched away Kutner in his big-throated prime.
You starry sentinels above, teach us to swim the serpentine channels of your
Tarry sands, searching for sign, sticky with misery's mystery.

Thing and All

I don't exactly think I will.
I don't exactly wish I don't.
The science is inexact, and don't
Think it won't splice you
As you swish by
On your two-stroke motor
Scooter with your bright visor
Held aloft for all to topple.
Your orbit is unseeming.
It takes you in, like a market
Spilling futures
On the livestock you are
On the soybeans you aspire to
And the hulls and straws
Baking your energy
Into meticulous kitty litter crypto-
Currency in the metabolic
Cycle you were born for:
Come and see yourself
By and by, baby-naked
And time-begrimed
In your coin-op space scope.
Its azimuth is lacking.
Its optics, unexacting
Can smother grainy eggs
Of the tiniest horned reptile
Secreted in the streambed
You once took to.
It might feel like something
To feel something capturing you
In milled mirroring lenses
As you are and would be
But that self-love
Is nostalgia.

Cape Cadaver

Basic bike
Mechanics come handy for clock-punching
Chanticleers: Enchained
In dinged dog tags, doubled-up, dentally
Forsaken and freely
Fretting the aforementioned fix.
Gingerly, a green gash halves
Hector's headset
At none's behest, hoisting a jackknife
Up his bejeweled rear axis, injurious
To old gents; just so,
Keyed-up kingdom-killer
Larry launches from his listening post
A delicate lash. Medical marvels arrive, muchachos
With immaculate masts
Nodding through the curdled night, puffed
With potency. Passing the patch kit
Unrequitedly through quizzical
Fingers, a queer resonance
Radiates in the nether reaches, the Reich.
Succotash Stan steps in, stout boatswain, struggling
To sight terra firma but twiddling
His twelve-ton tiller
In a vast vacant breeze and veering
Westward, there is no wrong way
Exactly to cross the extravagant
Zone of good fear with its hazardous souk, its shaming bazaar.

Zane Grey

Poster Boy for postprandial postnasal drip
Deposits posterior on mildewy post,
Posting bond. His *Judge*,
Post-nap, reposes unopposed
Beneath the proprietary *Personals* page
Of a spiky *Evening Post*,
Awakened from visions of postcoital
Postures of yore in *Señor*'s compostable
Post-and-beam chambers.
Then passes a *Postman* pausing his sack
Against a keening lamppost and
The whole unwholesome outpost inhales.
This is no duchy for postmortems
—Not while the *Prisoner* (that pest) prattles
For rough justice, whose imposition
Hizzoner's frowzy robes may no more postpone.
"Dispositive proof proffered by empurpled
Deposition supports the *Courtly* supposition
That the preposterous polecat
Poised before us poses
No positive twitch to *Property* or *Peoples*"
(Postulates the gavel swinger),
"And must be sprung, posthaste."
At this the portly *Bailiff* rouses
His clay from a posthypnotic
Pastoral, mounts the portico and puffs
A few putative notes of voluntary
Fanfare on his post horn.
"All rise, *Impostors, Pastors, Plasterers*,
Placard-Benders, Punk Policers,
And fly this dusty hoosegow, pronto.
(P.S. my *Horse* died.)"

Relief on all sides.
The ex-*Accused* recuses himself,
Clutching a spray of pansies
And putting pen to two-penny postcard—
Posthumous cadences
Pilfered poetastefully
From a tinny passel of Post-it notes.
Post hoc mockery shall await the *Fellow*
At the over-wrought penitentiary gate
With opposing thumbs and PTSD.
"Psst," he posits, summoning his *Sheriff*
For a final fondle of the *Lawman*'s uncocked pistol;
Then supposed he'd better'd not.
Postlapsarian, he loves a good fall.
Impossible posterity promises
The sight of *Himself*
On a *Wanted* bill, or at least the pleasant
Pinch of a baleful suppository;
Our venerable postage stamp agrees.

Porfirio Díaz

Porfirio Díaz was a master builder
Railways, bridges, aqueducts, dams
Tunnels, telegraph, power plants, canals
Electrification, irrigation, sanitation
Deepwater ports, seawalls, shipyards, ice
Breakers, steel-hulled trawlers
Public gardens, amphitheaters, windswept
Arenas, obelisks, monuments
To heroes of the revolution
Prisons, hospitals, armories
Steel mills, sawmills, cultivated expanses
Devouring the horizon
Where once darkest forests swarmed
Reclaimed swampland, mangrove
Bear his memory, his breath
He was a master marksman, frozen
Dawn in a moldering treestand
Above verdant stillborn Xochitlán
A gatherer of textiles, gimcracks
Faceted white glass and polished beads
Incisors, canines, mandibles, dead eyes
Pursuing him through sleep, Díaz
On horseback, in a mule cart, on foot
He strode as if through a stone passageway
Spat out by history to guide the peasantry
Along a thousand byways, purebred
Stream of unknown parentage
Furtive spokesman of the native tongue
With its whistled vowels and insinuations
Mountain-child, herder, sentry, machete-swinger
Steward of underground springs, purveyor
Of tonics, hallucinogens, Porfirio Díaz

Purple-robed, capturing the henequen trade
With Chinese field hands, capturing stores
Of Chilean gems, British bullion, African
Propellants in mine shafts, in catacombs
The production of copper went mad
Under him, landowners marched
Toward oblivion, indigenous practices
Prospered uneasily, musicians trailed him
With woodwinds and cannon-like trumpets though
He danced clumsily with his maimed leg
When his wife died he married her sister
Porfirio Díaz, or her sister's daughter
Fighting France, he was eulogized in France
Hair and sideburns trimmed
Polished with palm oil, laid in state
With pistols, naked daggers, a studded
Death mask of onyx and shale
Later repatriated by Empress Esmerelda
At Veracruz, or Catarina at Puebla who had loomed
Over him a foot or more, he had to balance
On a stool when he kissed her neck
When they swam off the Oaxacan coast
Near Puerto Escondido, out of sight
Of lackeys, bracing each other underwater
When a dolphin leapt toward them
When a wave snapped on them, snapping
Their necks but they swam on

Without Robinson

To whom do we refer, Robinson,
When we refer to you?
The sky above you offers
No reference, nor do the shambling barrens
Below, nor the undeciphered trimmings
We scrounged from your
Circumference.
What word, Robinson?
Yesterday's randy boy
Leaps over the meadow
In mad pursuit of you, tripping
Into the hay's hump,
The opening we fear: Down there
Is no interference, no
Boozy buffer interrupting
Transfer to our further shore;
Where Mama wades deep in the dirt and defers
To wormy inference, hunger, drear;
Where Pops, old sufferer, has declined
His heavy parcel. "I never saw the man himself"
Is his way of putting it in indifferent
Wrecked Greek. See here, Robinson,
You were born to the middle state,
The upper station of low life, and you bear
Origin in your midsection like
A middling manager of human resources
At a cast-off parts maker
—Bolts, clips, dowels, fasteners
Brackets, clasps, despised wrenches
Bent midway through your
Assembly; and the thing
You pound together looks like

Exactly nothing. That's your affair,
The furtive, infirm, fury-wracked
Leathery reek of your weakness for weakness.
Somewhere you wrest a tuber into daylight
After long struggle; elsewhere you confer
Upon your footwear a preference
For friction and chicken-steps.
Abiding your corner, cured by sun
Is how we know you when we find you
Stretched like a tarp to load our goods
And drag them ashore, when
We have no goods because
Demand for our kind is dead.

Delight in Disorder

Then the Governor dressed us down, then disordered
Grunts were, like body odors, disclosed. In wanting us,
He spread us on the sloping lawn, shoulder to shoulder,
And the skeet shooting above us was no distraction
For we were facedown in a deserving place.
I got a stomachache right then, and got myself
Into downward dog, a pair of thugs scuffling
Steel toed behind me. Up on stage, ribbony
Copper wavered while the keynote
Speaker did his droning best, petty, coated in rice flour:
A homegrown act, thrown up on a shoestring, but I
For one was done with ersatz civility.
The Governor leaned toward me, pursed his lips and farted.
Side by side, there was no telling apart which finger was whose.
He called me "Sweet Lady"
And the sun slipped across the moon like kindling and the wind
Held its yellow breath as he examined the back of his throat
With my cock. It was fine to be of every use.
There followed a snack of herring and toasts
With crimson butter and did I thereby
Neglect (full belly and all) to see one must
Not confuse legal possession with ownership
Of the bewitched lad's soul? "You have a winning smile,"
He praised. "It makes up, almost, for your tempestuous
Entrails." Well stretched out, I could no more care less
What words were, rolling about in the swale of wildflowers
Among living thorns and pollinators.
"Precisely," responded my scissors.

The Vine

ICE agents slip on a scab Ollie's
Dad sent back, booked for passing germs.
It's all I won't bear. Wheezy ally,
The tale my garlicky fluvia
Tell Fortune of shark meat is
Dimwitty. She in mid-juice
Met very untoward end. Nails
My spy over there seeded make
Bad for mule's health; illicit bums,
All in it up the windward sod,
Bleed rare beef, the finest cut.
For many quick ages there strove
Ghost pups, and pups maimed by Time's spend-
Y rural toy punks. Yes: lending a
Mammal an ample chimera
To address our love's belly is
A challenge. Base lodge is closed.
But then, I'm excited that the police
Dog went rabid and sicced rescuers: Inert,
Useless, wise Nature reels. I go now,
Paddling the scary dismal potted
Astroturf channels. I'll be on time
To tell if the black mortar in me lacks slime.

///

Dire Offense

Blasting his fusty clarinet
Above trench coat and hairnet
Was the twittering signal maker's call to order
Of his personal border
Guard, its mobile cannons and chew toys.
Just then, a thicket of Jewboys
Entered our crosshairs, territorially,
Like majestic reptiles conspiratorially
Frozen in a camouflaging cactus
Grove in a rictus
Of pure blood fever.
Me, I'm no believer
In holding fire, but the wall ran thick with Spanish
Moss in the likeness of ghostly mannish
Creepers and aromatic
Birdcalls: We picked up essences of razor wire, plasma, cinematic
Sinus pressure
And canal gouging, hot-to-the-touch Russian dolls, asset seizure,
Ceremonial shackles and so on.
Go on,
Said our man, clutching a list of hunter
Types available for target practice. A digital counter
Kept track of us
And our clammy bodies, lord knows there was no lack of us.

To put a finer spin on

It, we offered finespun pinions

To our comradely hijackers

(Highhanded they were, the bushwhackers)

But were turned crudely down.

That was before the great down-

Turn, before scuffed-up scavenging

Muckers appeared on our knoll with avenging

Barrows stacked at attention

In a salute of grandiose abstention:

Petty officers extolling privates, colonels

Shaking down seamen for scant kernels.

Bleeding gums or no, a little scarcity

Does a sailor good in the holy city,

Zings his leaky capacitor to the garters.

I must not now tell you we are lazy martyrs

On whitewashed deck chairs cracking a pistachio,

Licked by breezes and loosening our lips in a show

Of bodily danger

To pirates and pie cutters. Then comes a stranger

To fix our hard stare

Then comes a gut-flash: Where are our fair

Footsteps in the drowned wood now? Ours was a home

Birth; home is Stockholm.

The Rape of the Lock
Was a favorite pastime in times of lock-
Down, when, for instance, one of our number
Smuggled in poppers for all, leaving us number
Than snow-blind ice fishers
Searching for shore among zagged fissures;
Or when some random munitions-heavy assassin
Interrupted quiet time to break our asses in
With a christly urge to mutilate.
We hunkered in our remotest rec room till late
In the history of man and his/her germy console,
Like disconsolate
Souls who are done talking.
This returns me to the theme of the Baron stalking
Belinda's crazing coif with a two-edged sharpy
His trusty harpy
Clarissa slipped him and he snipped
So good; while swarming nymphs nipped
His itching parts like pit bulls
And lathered his frock with spit. "Bulls-
Hit—" expelled protestant inner Belinda, who shared
With the Baron a confidential spasm—"I am sheared
To the nape!"—then bleats like a spring lamb at us
In cadences calamitous.

"Thus far both armies to Belinda yield"
Sod-like. Then Dad blacks out and me, I feeled
Her up, because why not. She freaks: "Who invades
This state?"—and goes at me in sharpened spades
Digging me a new one. I would have died
Right now and been reborn a mole rat, pride
Of amorous pretenders, figurehead
Royale; but Trig, the brother, comes to spread
Me open in Belinda's nasty robe
In darkness, all upending the snow globe
On her night table, going at a pace
All businesslike. He shows but half his face,
Then calls in Carlos, his swart friend. Combined
We go like four, five times. I'll never find
Friends like those boys no more. You should have seen
Belinda when she finds us: She goes green,
Starts bawling, plunges straight in. Then in runs
Dad, roused from slumber, honking, "Christ, my sons!"
One son climbs off. "Look, Dad," he points, "your fly
Lies open," and we laugh till we would die.
The old man takes two steps, then starts to fall
In heaps on heaps. A second later, all
The EMTs are on him; but their art
Is no match for a bastard's flatlined heart.

Time Fate Love Beauty Power Ill-Nature Steel
Muse Goddess God Jove Neptune Hermes Sol
Ulysses Dido Proculus Propitious
Megrim Maeander Cynthia Thalestris
Sylph Sylphid Nymph Gnome Zephyretta Umbriel
Fay Fairy Pam Poll Ixiom Ace Ariel
Brillante Damon Dapperwit Clarissa
Sir Plume Sir Fopling Florio Crispissa
Belinda Betty Basto Partridge Spleen
Your Grace Imperial Consort Tyrant Queen
Imperial Courtier Star Knave Baron Lord
Chief Monarch Majesty Trump Matadore
Battalion Throng Guard Squadron British Throne
Force Troop Militia Nation Earth Heavens Moon
Sky Sea Land Desert Cave of Spleen Elysia
Rome China Afric Amazon Troy Asia
The Thames The Mall Home Grotto The Exchange
Fiend Phantom Specter Hero Personage
Jew Moor Host Merchant Judge Saint Infidel
Plebeian Politician Wretch Slave Female
Prude Virgin Harlot Belle Wife Virago
Hysteric Wise Man Vain Man Statesman Fellow
Mankind Imperial Race Fop Witling Heir
Soul Victor Victim Lover Ravisher

Playing at violence with sharpened sticks is delaying

Onset of incipient male horror, saith the experts. Once at

Recess on the dirt patch, you see, our boy wrests

Weapons from beneath his blouse, shouting, "Capons:

Dare challenge my might and I shall cut you where

Sensible fingers cannot reach and ostensible

Protectors, feeble, turn away." We had been studying Hector's

(Homer's) exploits: How the hero takes on comers

Brutally, blindly, operatically, beautifully

Defenestrating them; virility degenerating

(Alas) into a fervor to harass

Tormentors weak and strong, and to seek mentors

Best equipped to put boy's charms to a manly test.

Crises with Community-Standard-Bearers ensued; prices

Were paid and plans of recompense were laid.

Dad and I went apologetically along, but were inwardly proud.

Boys are marvelous when they master human toys.

Desire yearns to hold a boy to oneself like a prior

Self, untamed, ignited and moving with stealth,

Dumbly swerving like a beam from inner womanly

Stuff; and I confess I speak in part as one. I've had enough

Hard hands on me from early on to know the reward

Youthful initiation heaps on one's self's myth, truthful

Peon; surveying the play pit hither and beyond.

We rose from morning prayers
This morning tactically refreshed, like fresh-faced bombardiers,
When happening on a troupe of loitering chess player
Types encamped on paving stones in the town square
Right and left we kicked their whittled pieces afield with rare
Ritualistic aplomb—such was our sunrise state of rapture—where-
On one sallow chess-fancying elder scoured a flower bed for his errant knight
Piece, waving the recovered wreckage before us: And a blooming height
Of risk to the old-timer's self it was, for Simon, our oaf, raring
To gnash all and any profaners, stood staring
Down the geezer who in his sandals buckled but did not retreat
No did not: And with one forearm thwack fell to bits at Simon's feet,
Skulking on aged fours toward his far-flung chessman which our beefy boy reached first
And trod beneath boot. Stymied, the codger forthwith cursed
Semi-toothless oaths at us, and neither his withered mates nor our upright
Klatch of strapping homies betrayed awe at the sudden sight
Among us of clay pipes, chains, a blade or two, well-worn bricks, a crowbar,
While as for me my palm took rousing friction from a length of rebar:
Inciting a pageant of men's bodies in intimate downright
Mingling of dirt and mortal fluids after a long symbolizing night
Of prayer and chess play: Our side swept the board
Of pawns but could not grab the royal pair, as discord
Worked its wire into us: Revived, the antique gent caught Simon with a gory
Righteous hammer upraised: Nor would I deny him his glory.

After we miscalculated
The situation escalated
Calling for stern regulation
Of the client's simulation.
Woodlands, once defoliated
Henceforward accumulated
Grubs, worms and borers, as speculation
Re: "sundry violation
Of lawns and flower beds" grew, belated-
Ly, and sedation was slated
To ease nighttime installation
Of ventilation
Ducts. Our pincers, thus elated
Obliged the user, and freighted
Measures were enforced: Immolation,
Chokehold, deep knee bends, oscillation
Of old hardware and reticulated
Knobs. We inhaled and postulated
Our sponsor—the fretful consolation
Seeker—in his isolation
Suite. Tips bleached, eyes dilated—
(How sweetly his houseplant undulated)—
Our latest-born unloveliest relation,
Chief minister of stamp cancellation.

Stiffness and swelling of the joints
And shallow, labored breathing: Points
Worth taking to account when hiring
A houseboy. Seeking a retiring
Sort, I distributed bright flyers
To clinics—shelters—wherever fleers
From war and famine, for example,
Were tightly packed: Yielding an ample
Laboring pool that could be had
For a fair price, or none. Jihad-
Ists (former) were among them, hollow
Lads, versed in discipline and following
Commands and getting down to work.
I called the one I chose "Old Turk"
Though he was neither. "Turk," I called,
"Prithee, Old Turk," as I lay sprawled
In my tight nightshirt that first dawn,
Musing; then, with a feral yawn,
The lights cut out and a pair of hands
Fumbled in my folds. All lands
Must need remind us now that proper
Coupling is grounded in property
Rights: Neutral, bathed in silks and best
Served room temp at the customer's behest.

Poetry issues from our rough-made bed
Jet fuel–like, as Florio's heavy tread
Spies the unconscious subject's indifferent
Repose and *stop* In ranks, the nymphs' fervent
Militia braces for crusade, collapses
On naughty Damon *stop* who soon relapses
Entranced by cagèd swallow's silver sound
Don't Basto's thumbs are flexed on her—renowned
Therapy for Lady's chronic joint pain—crazing
His jeweled gloves up moonlit mystic mazing
Paths *please* Eager combatants gather round
High ramparts *no* besieging *no* boggy ground,
While Diana wafts upon a swift transition
And *swooning* goes dark, straining our position
Unto a feathered chaise of muttered cravings
—Recorded in the ledger as the *ravings*
Of Phoebus, fevered, and his sunburnt mind:
Who sleepwalks home *all done* snugly to bind
His secret in a locket. Planets *recede*,
Walls fall, great trees *bow down*; accounts concede
A bare lightbulb, upended flowers, more
Galloping clouds dying in metaphor
While Dapperwit, Sir Fopling and Sir Flume
Extrude Crispissa's soft unfading bloom.

We dare not speak for Mama's fetus
In the mother tongue, nor shall our censor entreat us
With his truncheon. We must keep wits
To ourselves as we keep, mostly, tits
Alert in all directions, vulnerable
Fleshy boxes that we are, vulgar rabble
Muzzling the workday through without a piss
To empty us. Nota bene: Bliss
Mingled with loathing serves up entitlement
As we gather rocks atop the battlement.
It's who I am is a motherfucker
Morning glory cocksucker
On the Trojan side of town on a science-based
Diet of stony self-evidence. Based
On our notes a dry-eyed fuck
Mightn't take the edge off Oklahoman and Kanuck,
Tuckahoe, Congressman, Cuff, transcender
Chieftain of intransigent transgender
Offenders. It pains us not to say our cunt
Shall hold the cursèd fast to account
For his arctic diversity
Of misdemeanors, and for the gift of adversity
His perversity bestows on us. "Complicit"
Is the full-term term; tasty shit.

Me with my lazy mouth

And habits of uncouth

Elocution

And habits of smearing lotion

In easy-to-reach recesses

Where cold compresses

Are a stevedore's way of life.

Don't tell his wife

He up and died

Inside

Atop the angel's cargo bed

While she (the wife) was biding time at head

Quarters, counting forward and back to a hundred and one.

By then he was done

Offloading, and that's what she gets leaving her grappling hooks

Untended, turning away to balance books

And put affairs in order

In order that the little murder-

Ing thief be got in the act: I saw him taken down

Like the too-personal pronoun

He wished to god not to answer to.

Turns out he had a touch of cancer, too.

—As don't we all, my now and ever lover,

Have a stage 4 case of Nothing to discover.

You can't say it that way with that word

You prove it by being it, coward

In the cellar atop your designated mound, lowered

In thought, fast-forward

To sizing your inseam with Uncle's forged sword

Not disemboweling, nor deflowered

Like a ward

Of the bespoke hayfield, its ur-weird

Collocation of hogs and medicinal worts, hartwort, woundwort

Afterward we gathered our wayward

Galoshes to peel off in a disempowered

Yank, habit hardwired

And etched in sorrow, awkward

Messengers we were, so where'd

We get that wart

On our bum, I could have sweared

Oaths to the wearied

Migrant among us, criminal blabbermouth, steward

Of earthward

Arrows hurtling dysphasically toward unanswered

Parts. What did we wish we ever were, duh

—Skewered

On a briny slip, like untoward

Dental plates, keepers of an inward password

All prior claims aside, our champion
Is as nameless-blameless as the soft gray
Skeleton that sleeps within us,
King of clams; and why it smarts so
To say so is a marvel for goldsmiths
To whack their tool at. Vaughan here, for one,
Would not say no to a proper suckling,
Some toothy chew of plump pope's nose
Downed with a loveless chaser; his crew,
Too, lodged in a crabbed corner, gnashes
Its lanyard like a fizzed-up dispenser and
Christ we're due for a crash. "Awe-
Some child, come toddle your gas can,"
Sighs Sidney, the eldest, pinching a kidney.
But the rally has taken a sorry turn,
"And anyway" (grouses Old Gay), "fuck groveling."
Reamed by Milton, we cave on Shirley's bed,
Awaiting our swift sherbert and pasting back
Cowlicky tresses with a wet comb like
A good chap. Man-on-man contests follow
(One cow per entrant) and the backed-up john soon
Flows gently south. Well put: A more lowdown
Dire note never issued from other rickety hi-fi;
Till all song ceases and the last yellow cake is done.

Ping-pong manifesto predatory impasto gum chewing crack
Smacking fume burglar flycatcher filibuster nosedive Iraq
Whacking hot snuff chain clangor fresh funk pencil rebel
Stubble farmer godawful cartwheel teleprompter nasal rubble
Able-bottomed fishmonger finger merchant toadstool lewd
Brooder bung stump fleece leash interdental sapsucker fluid
Dude cold front migratory comet slime hortatory Warsaw
Seesaw Percodan perjury nuke node piddle poof T cell rickshaw
Outlaw ash basting acid mallet varnish vendor flagellant
Flatulent spatula sorceress null set tick tock whirligig accelerant
Elephant recipient minibar bath oil nipple scrub software
Elder care load bearing tramp spanker bark sculpture Delaware
Bus fare refugee pollyanna nightingale clock bait polygraph
Staph infection insurrection spoon licking cheese puff life raft
Riff raff polyrhythmic chipped beef pederasty tin can Istanbul
Forkful antiseptic contraceptive tractor pull teeny bopper landfill
Melville hypnogogic snow blow ass sniff civic crater promenade
Homemade pomade cave-creeper missionary frostbite alimony lemonade
Stun grenade ferry man gas can rat catcher xbox Nova lox Cape Town
Uptown masking tape sober tuber rubber necking crowbar shakedown
Surround sound static cling plum picker musketeer pioneer
Puppeteer grog slugging tonsil swab dildo dingo auctioneer
Tin ear skin flinting starburst Shylock ziplock mickey-slipping tailor
Jailer patricidal butterfly two-legged isotope corn starch sterilizer

The little box
Came home with me, locks
And all. Unable
To clear suitable
Space, I set
It in a cabinet
In my crap toolshed
Strewn with dead
Batteries and twisted
Nails that resisted
Straightening out.
Could I doubt
The box contained
An old complaint?
It stunk
Of dead grass, funk.
There was no prying
It open or trying
Gingerly to shatter
It; no matter
What I did I
Failed. Did I
Use force?
No, of course.

Rapacious maneuvers in conquest and escape
Cut a crepuscular
Path through our pre-Raphaelite shrapnel-
Seeded grounds, and find us draped
Beneath a regal serape
In a grape-bursting family way. Our raptor
Rappels from on high like a bloodflower tapering
Toward our lapel
Rapier-like, there to be secured by staple
Gun: Repellant child, imitating a papier-
Mâché ape,
Gap-toothed, having traipsed
Oceans in search of a vaporized
Drunk bunkmate; that is to say, "a penguin."
Such are the capitulating terms of our caper,
Human enough to make a Lady gape
Over her morning crêpe
And dewberry frappe;
And such a one was our lapis
Lazuli–bearing trapeze-
Slinging Belinda, with her ripe gripes
And feints of rapid rapture.
We cracked her carapace
In twos; the thing's on tape.

Jim, I don't believe this action.
Linda had an overripe reaction
To dust, and dumbass Ned put in a panicked call
To Ronny's Paramedics, who are in the downstairs hall
Right now hurling axes. Kim pretends a seizure for distraction's
Sake, but Fireman Russ, no fool, makes a tactician's
Lunge at the kitchen screen door, finding Mary
Pacing the pavers out back with Dad's stun gun held high, scary
Thought: Christian, dim soul, does his best to talk her down
In silken tones, but no go. Meanwhile Barry is going to town
On a pale shadow on the dewy lawn, observed by Stud,
Our rescue dog. Elsewhere Jen and Sue linger in the mud
Beneath a jacaranda, snuggling, unaware little Mackey is
Prowling Old Miss Putnam's fence with his khakis
Hitched high. Ahmed spies him there and delivers
A well-placed kick to the lumbar, while Becca shivers
Nearby in the dead lettuce patch, forgetting the name (Raúl)
Of the guy she and Jared led home from school
Who lies between them now, not quite conscious. Suzette
And Trevor await sunrise through a pastel cigarette
Haze, supine on the roof with sweaty Pam.
Stars fade, Linda's yowls subside, car doors slam.
Trig, the creep next door, dares us to say boo to him.
What of it? Sound good? Up for a nightcap, Jim?

Somebody

Down on the body shop

Floor ought to keep his body

To himself, or might catch himself in a foreboding

Headlock in this greasy abode.

Passing round his rusted-out axle for anybody

To take turns working on won't bode

Well for repair of his manual parts; nor will robotics

Do a hardbody

Any favors when his jalopy is jonesing like nobody's

Business to unlace its steel bodice

And take a lap or two in Miss Peabody's

Demolition derby, where a healthy body slam

Shall be memorialized by body cam

For prying eyes: And an onerous bodacious

Effort it will be to rehang his mashed-in frame on its bodiless

Chassis, as he drifts disembodied

In a lavender cloud of B.O.

Down the aisles of the bodega

Where he hauls his shamed junk.—You'd think a homebody

Like him would have grown a pair of antibodies

By now to fend off busybodies?

He's nobody's bodhisattva.

These old bones speak bad body English.

To give you a picture of us
In those luminous
Days before your arrival, consider the trap
We were apt
To lapse into back then, like our belief
In the salving chemical properties of touch, offering relief
From toothache, earache, heartache, tantrums, quakes and relief
From strays like you, old husk, seeking climax in grief.
Yours was a ritual of circulating
Winds and ululating
Tongues spilling vowels.
Your sky was all intactness, your conscience scrubbed, nocturnal howls
Went unclaimed
Or were ascribed to unnamed
Bodies darting past you this way and that, sinking
In muddy boreholes their stinking
Pit-a-pat. We listened for you elsewhere
In mine shafts, flooded fields and dells where
We gathered to confront
The slaughter of the African elephant
And hide its trumpet where we may be found: The grieving creature
Moans to the furthest reaches
And treads round its lover's bones
Permanently alone.

Los Toritos

When the little bulls, so-called, rained down
From passing rainclouds like little bullets
Unexploded, wishing only
To scrub themselves away on their armored backs
In postures of surrender;
When we, trainees, young men and boys
With imperfectly formed morals, flipped them
Onto their sticky ridged bellies
With wooden spoons, then nudged them
Toward the drylands, only to return
Hours later from evening drills
To find them back on their backs,
Pedaling crooked limbs like antique toys
About to wind down, to snap shut the turnkey
Driven deep in their bellies;
When the bony concrete verandah
Of our bungalow and those of the empty adjacent
Bungalows from which wind radiated
Were speckled suddenly with dull pools
Marking the end of dry season
And the pools swam with upended little bulls
Who could not be made by any means to go on living
And even crows
Stayed away from them, even the militant beady ants
Who had risen from the ground
Would not strip their remains
Or carry them away
In opalescent flakes, no, well by then
We had finished our drills
And were moving on. Done with mandatory tasks,
Done polishing
The ceremonial scalloped horns

That marked us for what we were,
The little language we got by on
Wasn't much but was enough
To carry us down the ravine,
And solids and liquids had passed through us
While the living leaves and flowers had stopped needing us.
Dogs and pushcarts, whirring children, motorbikes, vans
In the rutted paths, there was
No asking what woke us
In the rain, what morning today was,
What destination. Some ornamental
Piece off our wrist had been
Snatched, a bracelet or timepiece,
As we awaited our lift,
Some piece from our pack had been sold off,
Some other piece in us had misgivings
And went back inside where things
Of questionable being go.

On Himselfe

The workers' movement is, first off, dead.
Workers' rights, it turns out, were a scam.
"Isn't it a fine thing I
Done," we asked our hairy hands back when
Young countries like ours busied themselves collecting blackest
Men to fend off death-work: The disintegrating wear
And tear of feeding oneself bonemeal, rinds, shucks and such swill
Maidens and knights left behind—retiring muses—
Setting down robes in fountains and getting ready to breathe
Upon our foreheads. Our Lady of Servitude, for one, she'd
Mystify us in her blather atop her cube,
Curl fetally, leak blood.
The thing to do was ignore her, resume tending my
Myrtle and mulching my seedbeds and throwing back a fizzy pale Pacífico if
Corona's not available. Comfort
Washed over us then with its debilitating thesis:
With a stroke of the spade, a carburetor, with
Sweet neglect of all norms but
Ointments and hot wraps; we took our martyrdom
Thus, casually cruel, not like the machinist who muses
Atrociously over pricky details. So the
Last I heard my people were stuck on a train.
Indeed it takes a cattle car to suffer
Comedians and commandants who divide laborers into
Two straggling classes of vermin. Still we come,
Suffering dust, fungus, sterilizing salts, though I
Insisted after showering this would be the last
The bastards would handle us like that.
Muses instructed us to raise hatchets to Boethius.
Martyrdom clogged the streets and no ointments
Buttered us back to wholeness. For a while we got sweet
With the help but who could trust one's fingers with

This insurrection going on. After the sheets were washed,

Comfort brimmed from the neighbor boy's chocolate coronet—

If only he would stop stalking Myrtle,

My girl, whom we found in Emergency with the

Blood beneath her fingernails and sawdust in her curls.

Believe me it gets worse. Gamy

Shepherds were rounded up on

The orders of the foreman and his surly set—

Muses, magicians, landlords—wielding implements made in

Willful disregard of orifices, waving fire and

Wearing vengeful armor streaked with semen.

Blackest centuries passed when the word was young

When work at hand was done.

I can face my kind and yours but answer me this:

Am I wrong to insist ours is work

Dead folk perform on each other down in Lethe?

Data

Taliban troubadours in livid knit
T-shirts trundling afield, ears bent
To the countryside: Monumental mead
Trilling with marmot, cricket,
Detonating blackbirds flushed from a felled
Tulip tree and distant
Drums finger-rattled by foot
Troops. It's lunchtime; quiet
Time to tally, rally, reflect,
Twist twine, chomp seed;
Tintinnabulating throat-calls hushed.
Ten dimes to a buck: two stones: eight
Tawny eggs: a pound of brown bread
Divvied up triangularly like cow's heart
Doused with a cold rivulet
To quench our pad
-Dy and water our twitchy beast.
Displaced algae drift
Decorously on a silvered pond
Downstream; reluctant mist
Drops in our midst
Dreamlike, like profit.
Ten minutes pass, then a long sought
Temblor comes and forthwith comes and
Disperses tourists to the mazy market
Tent with its deft
Tipping of a handcart
—Tire irons, thumbtacks, tar pails, cement.
Toothache doesn't mat-
Ter in a windstorm in the minaret:
Tendon-flexing doesn't rank: Gut
Trauma is a knot
Daylight drops through a trapdoor in its strict
Desire for no child-bearing artifact.

Auto

Now we had thrown our lot in
With Bill and Carlotta, benders of the books
At the GM-Jeep-Mercedes-Saab lot
On the scrubbed hilltop overlooking Mormon Trek
With its flotilla of vulcanized
Hard-anodized well-tempered units
Heaving in port, unpiloted—
Now our noonday trot
Had got round the treatment facility
Where elder brother Tod
Lay in long-term hold
In the stability bay with his flock of aging
Mallets and chimes—
Now our reflection had been caught
In a blinding pond beside the cottage
With an overwrought handyman
Whose work gloves we had happened on
On our sundown ramble across the woodlot
Without regret—
Now, even now our zealotry had softened
In a merlot-stained hush, as we lustered
Semi-clothed, sipping dark jars
In our checkerboard housing slot
In our shady allotment
With circuit breaker, carport, lotus-
Heavy garden plot roiling
With eggplants and insect-bitten
Lettuces, and nighttime's winch
Came closing in on us
And the rotating moon
Came dropping its heat in our envelope—
While seabirds raised caws and distant

Glottal cries, blotting out
Sky with quickened wingbeats and a rain
Of riotous skylarks, falcons, impalas, jaguars
Ocelots, splotchy colts
Loose on the littered lawn
Now, in our former state
In our current one
In stately procession
We may, we would, we might
We ought

The Vine

Diorama death some retail ape-rat-of-man
Owes my tumor up his idiot oven
Wha? Chicory woolen gun and Eve row
On the roll: doomed unto lice,
Am too high to hoe oral nugs O'Malley. Logos in death-goth's
Wet hue mute no odor oils, did Sir Porous
Hire blue labia? Attack, send her west
Boom! so fat no rival toes wear ember cud.
Obit hero hid weary thing-henge.
Endow the race he coils, trashed mini-ego
At halves, hurt me, please obey, o hang
Seth, Tim, Lucas, Mad Tom.
Eyeing abaci chase RV's head boy—his tree—
My cruel sea bather—in icy kiddo car AWOL
Under muse. I need hen dust hidden to hurl a lie
So that ash-cloud not for luster,
Ol' leper, taste her mud nap ire sooner.
Btw, hun-crap tweet halva is thud.
The spurt sea who chem-desk pine espied
Us chafe a lot on GOP loser's three-tiki
Oath to wee-too hoot hoofin' cow. OK,
No deafened home ethos of loose Haifa money.
Moor elk is to cook ethanol, Kevin.

His Poetrie His Pillar

Only sailors speak of pyramids
I left behind, back when I lived in hope.
Then as now, I sought to please
And betray, to be tightly buttoned up.
It is unkind, I know, to have handled you
That way, when your baubles were thrown
Or smashed for all to touch. Me
And my boys will turn to stone
Over time, not to worry. Easeful death
And neglect, acids and heavy rain will rot
Memorial statues and old bones beneath.
Often enough in Sunday School we forgot
How to use manners, for we were
Involved in heavily planning Dad's memorial
And had no idea how his mound got here
Without earth movers bearing down like a wall.
Behold (he warned us): Brute force eats away
Inch by inch unwelcome spirits within it.
Never, hearing his words, have we had a meal stay
Down so long, undigested, like minute
Caterpillars gathering into a glum circle. Goodnight—
If that's the way to say the kingdom's over.
Here it stood, wanting only to write
And vanish, Robert Herrick, nothing more.

"strange shadows on you tend"

There go another million minutes
   In the history of the misery
Of the nursery rhyme
   That puts our baby to bed
In a high bed at the end of time's
            White corridor.
There goes a voice, tripping over
Salutations, ostentations
  Today's recital of a day's rations
         Boiled potatoes, cream potatoes, black bread, rye
  In a woozy murmur
In a rose-throated hush
 Our ragged public address
 System lingers over.
It is a long caress
         Calling us home, come home
From chalked sidewalks, sloping shadows
               It is a bouquet of names
            A mother musters in a year of birth
                  Laura, Linda, Thomas, Gregory, James
Lost, long-sought
 Wine-dark interiors and rumors
Of warfare here and there
Among acres
 Of scattered wildlife, watery wastes.
         But if we do not come when called
            We'll have no supper, after all.
         But if we come home halfway round
            No one will be waiting up.
It will be as we have feared
  As day's end has neared
And a day's work left in its rainy place, stone work

Needlework, field and factory work

Transportation, trade, hard use

Mobs are spilling forward now

Onto barriers, Old Friend, onto esplanades

And dizzying

Pine groves and marshes

Down to a gauzy sea

We would return to as birds

Return, return.

Down there for what it's worth we shall recall

Our little duet

At the edge of ramparts

Thin sun parted us from.

We were counting up and down, we were

Stepping back in place

In a welter of words

Sayings, soundings, winded warnings, sighs

Exhortations, guttered silences and

Come close now.

It's time to listen in now.

Our cousin Amy B., psychiatrist once

Removed

Stranger to us is whispering to us

Of an antique man on the dying ward

Who cried and cried for his mother

A million years gone

"As all children do."

It is a tale told to passengers

Backseat of a vehicle

Careering through underpasses and channels the long way round

Our shortest visit.

The psychiatrist's mother

Beside me is crying and crying

For her mother, mother of mine

In an old winding verse

I am trying not to follow

God only knows, only knows

In the hour of his birth, Dear Friend

You wept for the old man our boy would be

Soon enough one day in a room

On a half-made bed

Attended

By no light

And would he look back toward us

Where we leave him

Rising from the thick-strewn forest floor shadow-crossed

Goodbye.

It is not that he was never here

Or that we were never here.

It's just, oh just that he and we

Have lost a way

Together

NOTES

THE FOLLOWING poems are modeled, in various ways, on poems by Robert Herrick, whose titles they share, and from which they adapt language and other elements: "The Vision," "The Argument of His Book," "To the Virgins, to Make Much of Time," "Delight in Disorder," "The Vine" (both versions), "On Himselfe," and "His Poetrie His Pillar."

"Dire Offense" uses some language from Alexander Pope's "The Rape of the Lock," from whose opening line its title is taken. In particular, the line that begins the section "Thus far both armies to Belinda yield" is from "The Rape of the Lock," canto III, 65, and the end words of the subsequent lines in Pope's poem (III, 66–88) are preserved throughout this section, sometimes homophonically. The section beginning "Time Fate Love Beauty Power Ill-Nature Steel" is comprised entirely of language from "The Rape of the Lock," and the section "Poetry issues from our rough-made bed" further uses and alters language from Pope's poem.

The section of "Dire Offense" beginning "We dare not speak for Mama's fetus" has two sources for fourteen of its end-words: George Carlin's "Seven Words You Can Never Say on Television" (1972) and the seven words that the U.S. Department of Health and Human Services reportedly directed the Centers for Disease Control and Prevention not to use in its communications as of December 2018 (https://www.nytimes.com/2017/12/16/health/cdc-trump-banned-words.html).

ACKNOWLEDGMENTS

MY THANKS TO the journals in which these poems appeared: *Bennington Review* ("Lark," "Bantam," "Porfirio Díaz"); *Denver Quarterly* ("Sacrificial," "Data"); *Gulf Coast* ("Delight in Disorder," "His Poetrie His Pillar"); *The Harvard Advocate* ("Untitled [Sir]," "Thing and All"); *The Iowa Review* ("Dire Offense"); *Lana Turner* ("The Argument of His Book," "To the Virgins, to Make Much of Time," "Without Robinson," "The Vine (I)," "On Himselfe," "strange shadows on you tend"); *Ploughshares* ("Los Toritos").

I am grateful to Lynne Nugent for publishing "Dire Offense" in its entirety. Chicu Reddy was a generous and attentive reader of this book.

Thank you to the people at University of Iowa Press, and in particular to James McCoy, Karen Copp, and Sara Sauers.

Emily Wilson is in all of this.